SPOTLIGHT ON SOCIAL AND EMOTIONAL LEARNING

YOU CAN FIX IT

SOLVING PROBLEMS

DAVID KLIMCHUK

PowerKiDS press.

New York

Published in 2020 by The Rosen Publishing Group, Inc.
29 East 21st Street, New York, NY 10010

Editor: Rachel Gintner
Designer: Michael Flynn

Photo Credits: Cover PeopleImages/E+/Getty Images; cover, pp. 1, 3–4, 6–10, 12, 14, 16, 18, 20, 22–24 (background) TairA/Shutterstock.com; p. 5 Sabphoto/Shutterstock.com; p. 6 Pressmaster/Shutterstock.com; p. 7 LightField Studios/Shutterstock.com; p. 8 Norb_KM/Shutterstock.com; p. 9 MediaNews Group/Getty Images; p. 10 Oleksiy Mark/Shutterstock.com; p. 11 Neirfy/Shutterstock.com; p. 12 Dirk Ercken/Shutterstock.com; p. 13 mrs/Moment/Getty Images; p. 14 Pop Paul-Catalin/Shutterstock.com; p. 15 JGI/Jamie Hill/Getty Images; p. 17 Jeff Holmes/PA Images/Getty Images; p. 18 Just Dance/Shutterstock.com; p. 19 Jupiterimages/Photolibrary/Getty Images; p. 21 Leon Bennett/FilmMagic/Getty Images; p. 22 Bo1982/Shutterstock.com.

Library of Congress Cataloging-in-Publication Data

Names: Klimchuk, David, author.
Title: You can fix it : solving problems / David Klimchuk.
Description: New York : PowerKids Press, [2020] | Series: Spotlight on social and emotional learning | Includes index.
Identifiers: LCCN 2019005179| ISBN 9781725307049 (pbk.) | ISBN 9781725307070 (library bound) | ISBN 9781725307056 (6 pack)
Subjects: LCSH: Problem solving in children--Juvenile literature. | Decision making in children--Juvenile literature.
Classification: LCC BF723.P8 K585 2020 | DDC 155.5/1343--dc23
LC record available at https://lccn.loc.gov/2019005179

Manufactured in the United States of America

CPSIA Compliance Information: Batch #CWPK20. For further information contact Rosen Publishing, New York, New York at 1-800-237-9932.

CONTENTS

CHAPTER ONE

FIXING THE PROBLEM

Have you ever had problems come up at school, at home, or out in your community? Have these problems ever left you feeling confused or **frustrated**? If so, you're not alone!

Every day, people deal with problems of all shapes and sizes. For some, their problem may be that they don't understand their math homework. For others, it might be dealing with the death of a loved one. No matter what problems you've had, you've probably found yourself wondering what to do. Maybe you've even felt a little hopeless. There are many different problem-solving skills that can help you break down the issue and improve the situation.

Problem-solving skills can be helpful for decreasing **stress**, improving relationships, and reaching your life goals. While a problem might have more than one possible **solution**, these skills will help guide you in the right direction.

Sometimes problems create stress and cause panic. In these moments, it's important to remember that everyone experiences problems and there are solutions at hand.

CHAPTER TWO

MAKING GOOD CHOICES

Solving problems is a key part of growing up and learning responsible decision-making. It's easy to act quickly and impulsively, or without thought, when we don't know what to do or if we're feeling scared. This sometimes makes the situation worse and doesn't get us closer to solving the problem. Responsible decision-making involves looking closely at situations, reflecting on them, and thinking about the consequences of our actions.

Taking time to think about a problem and a healthy way to solve it can help you make better decisions.

Learning skills for responsible decision-making can help you improve your life by decreasing stress and giving you something to be proud of. When you feel good about the decisions you make, you'll be more likely to keep making the right choices in the future. Becoming a good problem solver takes time, but the more you learn and the more you practice, the easier it will be.

CHAPTER THREE

CHECKING IN WITH YOURSELF

When we face a problem, we feel various emotions that change the way we think about the problem. When we feel our emotions taking over, it can be hard to stay calm. For example, if you found out that you're going to miss your favorite TV show because a family event came up, you might get very angry. If you calm yourself down, you'll realize you have other ways to see the show later. The first step in dealing with your emotions is to identify whether you're feeling sad, angry, scared, guilty, or a different emotion.

Pema Chödrön is a Buddhist teacher who encourages people to use breathing as a way to calm down and focus on the present.

Once you label your emotions, you can calm yourself down so you can solve the problem. One approach for this is called "grounding." You can do this by looking around and noticing things you see, hear, smell, touch, and taste. This can help clear your mind.

CHAPTER FOUR

WHAT TO SOLVE

Taking the time to ground yourself and become calm when facing a problem is important. Sometimes, when we take a second look at a problem, we realize it's very different than we thought. The problem can be easier to solve now that we feel in control.

It might be helpful to ask yourself: what, when, and where is the problem? Also, how is it happening and who's involved? Ask yourself the "who" question last because it can be very easy to jump into pointing fingers at people. You can ask friends and family these questions, too.

After you think about these questions, write a few sentences **describing** the problem as **specifically** as you can. The more **information** you gather about the problem, the easier it will be to come up with the best solution.

When you write them down, problems may seem a little more familiar—and maybe even easier to solve!

CHAPTER FIVE

WHAT CAN YOU DO?

Now that you've calmed down and figured out what the problem is, it's time to start coming up with solutions! The first thing to do is to come up with a list of as many ways forward as you can think of. Don't rule out any ideas or think about **obstacles** yet. Even if one of your ideas seems odd, put it on your list. Try not to get stuck thinking about what ideas worked or didn't work the last time you had a problem. Each situation is different. You can get ideas by turning to your family, friends, or teachers for advice.

After you have your list, go through and cross off the ideas that you know for sure won't work. Try to narrow it down to three or four options so that you have a few backup plans.

Thinking about obstacles sometimes makes us want to give up on solving our problems. Even if a problem seems impossibly hard, it's important to keep trying and working toward positive solutions.

CHAPTER SIX

PICKING THE BEST PLAN

Once you've gone through your solutions list and picked the top two or three choices, it's time to choose the best one to go with. After you decide which plan to use, hold on to the other ones in case you need a backup.

One way to make your final decision is to use a "pros and cons" sheet. Draw a line down the center of a piece of paper and write down all the good parts of the plan on one side and all the bad parts of the plan on the other. The plan with the most pros and the fewest cons might be the one to go with. However, not every choice is the best for every person. What works for your friend might not work for you based on your individual skills and strengths.

Sometimes, it takes a lot of thinking to make the best decision.

CHAPTER SEVEN

THE WORST THAT COULD HAPPEN

Getting ready to solve a big problem might be a little bit scary. You might have fears and **predictions** about what could go wrong. It's natural to have these fears when doing something new. One way to handle these fears could be by using the "**coping** ahead" skill. You can "cope ahead" by imagining yourself in the situation before it actually happens. Think about what emotions you might have in that moment and what you might do to handle them. Write down this plan and go over it again and again until you feel less scared and more **confident**.

For example, if you're nervous about taking a big test, imagine yourself in the classroom and think about how you might feel in that moment. Perhaps you'll be anxious and **tense**. Nevertheless, write down three ways to handle those feelings and practice them until it's not so scary.

You can also imagine the best that could happen in a situation! For example, soccer champion Carli Lloyd often imagines herself scoring goals on the soccer field before her games.

CHAPTER EIGHT

GIVE IT A SHOT

Now that you've created a list of solutions, narrowed them down, reviewed your pros and cons, and imagined the worst that could happen, it's time to put that plan in action. When trying your plan, it's important to be confident and respectful to others. Be sure to make eye contact and speak clearly and calmly. This helps you to feel better about yourself and to be taken seriously.

If your plan doesn't work at first, that's OK! That's why you have more than one backup plan. If you didn't reach your goal, go through your steps and think about what you could do differently. For example, your friend might not let you borrow a game if they have plans to use it. You might ask to borrow it another day.

Confidence is an important tool for being successful and being taken seriously when solving problems.

CHAPTER NINE

DID IT WORK?

How do you know if your plan worked? The first step is to check in with your emotions. Are you still having the same feelings, or has there been a change? Also, take another look at your original goal. Maybe somewhere along the way your goal has changed!

It's also helpful to observe how other people **responded**. Do they seem to be happy about the outcome? Let's say that your problem was that you and your best friend weren't getting along. You explained your side of things. If this worked, they might be smiling and laughing with you instead of frowning and yelling.

Sometimes we don't achieve our goals on the first try and we need to make some changes. Either way, we can learn a lot from the journey of solving problems and making mistakes along the way.

Don't give up on your goals! Comedian Jim Carrey was turned down many times early in his career, but he kept learning and growing until he achieved his goals.

CHAPTER TEN

OTHER WAYS TO SOLVE A PROBLEM

Just as there are many types of problems, there are many ways to solve them and make good decisions. Another way to approach a problem is to draw pictures of what's going on. A picture or **diagram** might help you figure out what's going on and why. Sometimes problems might need to be solved in the moment and you won't have time to plan things out. You just have to use your past experiences to find the best step forward.

Whether your problem is big or small, easy or hard, using your problem-solving skills of looking closely at a situation, imagining its outcome, and making a plan can go a long way. The more you think about your decisions and how they will affect others, the more likely you'll do something that makes you proud.

Always striving to do your best and working to find positive solutions will make you an awesome problem solver!

GLOSSARY

confident (KAHN-fuh-duhnt) Feeling that you can do something well.

cope (KOHP) To deal with and try to find solutions for problems.

describe (dih-SKRYB) To tell about in detail.

diagram (DY-uh-gram) A drawing that explains or shows the parts of something or how something works.

frustrated (fruh-STRAY-tuhd) Feeling angered or let down.

information (ihn-fuhr-MAY-shuhn) Knowledge or facts about something.

obstacle (AHB-stih-kuhl) Something that stops forward movement or progress.

prediction (prih-DIHK-shuhn) A statement about what will or might happen in the future.

respond (rih-SPAHND) To do something as a reaction to something that has happened or been done.

solution (suh-LOO-shuhn) Something that solves a problem.

specifically (spih-SIH-fih-kuh-lee) In a definite and exact way.

stress (STRES) Strong feelings of worry or anxiety.

tense (TENS) Nervous, not able to relax.

INDEX

PRIMARY SOURCE LIST

Page 9
Pema Chödrön. Photograph. Cliff Grassmick. October 5, 2014. Kept in the Digital First Media Collection on Getty Images.

Page 17
Carli Lloyd. Photograph. Jeff Holmes. November 13, 2018. Kept in PA Images Collection on Getty Images.

Page 21
Jim Carrey at a Golden Globes after-party. Photograph. Leon Bennett. January 6, 2019. Kept in Film Magic Collection on Getty Images.

WEBSITES

Due to the changing nature of Internet links, PowerKids Press has developed an online list of websites related to the subject of this book. This site is updated regularly. Please use this link to access the list: www.powerkidslinks.com/SSEL/solving